SO-AZH-559

42

JUAN PABLO MONTOYA

Superstars of
NASCAR

RIGHT
ON!

Marcy Wright

Gareth Stevens
Publishing

Please visit our Web site, www.garethstevens.com. For a free color catalog of all our high-quality books, call toll free 1-800-542-2595 or fax 1-877-542-2596.

Library of Congress Cataloging-in-Publication Data

Wright, Marcy.
Juan Pablo Montoya / Marcy Wright.
    p. cm. — (Superstars of NASCAR)
Includes index.
ISBN 978-1-4339-3960-0 (pbk.)
ISBN 978-1-4339-3961-7 (6-pack)
ISBN 978-1-4339-3959-4 (library binding)
1. Montoya, Juan Pablo, 1975—Juvenile literature. 2. Automobile racing drivers—Colombia—Biography—Juvenile literature. I. Title.
GV1032.M53W75 2010
796.72092—dc22
[B]
                                        2010007390

First Edition

Published in 2011 by
Gareth Stevens Publishing
111 East 14th Street, Suite 349
New York, NY 10003

Copyright © 2011 Gareth Stevens Publishing

Designer: Michael J. Flynn
Editor: Mary Ann Hoffman

Photo credits: Cover (Jaun Pablo Montoya), pp. 1, 25 Rusty Jarrett/Getty Images; pp. 4, 6, 8, 12, 14, 16, 18, 20, 24, 26, 28 (background on all) Shutterstock.com; pp. 5, 27 Geoff Burke/Getty Images; p. 7 David Maxwell/AFP/Getty Images; pp. 9, 10–11 Robert Laberge/Getty Images; p. 13 Scott Nelson/AFP/Getty Images; p. 15 Robert Sullivan/AFP/Getty Images; p. 17 Clive Rose/Getty Images; p. 19 Matthew Stockman/Getty Images; p. 21 Nick Laham/Getty Images; pp. 22–23 Marc Serota/Getty Images; p. 29 Chris Graythen/Getty Images.

Printed in the United States of America

CPSIA compliance information: Batch #CS10GS: For further information contact Gareth Stevens, New York, New York at 1-800-542-2595.

Contents

A Colombian Racer   4

Starting Young   6

Formula Racing   10

The Move to NASCAR   18

Helping Children   24

Timeline   30

For More Information   31

Glossary   32

Index   32

A Colombian Racer

Juan Pablo Montoya is a NASCAR driver. He is from the country of Colombia in South America.

Starting Young

Juan Pablo was born on September 20, 1975. He began racing when he was about 6 years old. By the time he was 9 years old, he was winning karting championships.

sparco
J.P. Montoya
TARGET
CHIP GANASSI
RACING
CART • FEDEX
CHAMPIONS
1996 • 1997 • 1998 1999

At the age of 15, Juan Pablo was racing and winning all over the world. He won the Kart Junior World Championship twice.

Formula Racing

By 1992, Juan Pablo was racing open-wheel, single-seat cars. These cars are used in formula racing.

Juan Pablo Montoya

Juan Pablo raced in the U.S. Formula racing series called the CART Championship Series. In 1999, he became the youngest driver ever to win the championship!

13

In 2000, Juan Pablo won a very famous formula race called the Indianapolis 500. He surprised many people because it was his first time in the race.

Juan Pablo moved to the top formula racing series—Formula 1. He won a big race called the Grand Prix (PREE) of Monaco in 2003.

17

The Move to NASCAR

In 2006, Juan Pablo decided to leave open-wheel racing. He became the first Formula 1 driver in history to move to NASCAR.

In 2007, Juan Pablo was named the Sprint Cup Rookie of the Year. That means he was the best first-year driver in the top NASCAR series.

At a race at the Daytona Speedway in 2008, Juan Pablo raced as part of a team. The team raced for 24 hours!

Helping Children

Juan Pablo and his wife help children in poor Colombian neighborhoods. They raise money to build places where children can play sports.

Juan Pablo and his wife hold a contest where children paint helmets for Juan Pablo. People bid for the helmets. The money goes to help other children.

Juan Pablo Montoya is famous in formula racing and NASCAR. Where will he race next?

Timeline

1975 Juan Pablo is born on September 20 in Colombia, South America.

1999 Juan Pablo wins the CART Championship Series.

2000 Juan Pablo wins the Indianapolis 500.

2003 Juan Pablo wins the Grand Prix of Monaco.

2007 Juan Pablo begins racing in NASCAR.

2007 Juan Pablo is named Sprint Cup Rookie of the Year.

For More Information

Books:

Greve, Tom. *Formula One Racing.* Vero Beach, FL: Rourke
    Publishing, 2009.

Kelley, K. C. *Hottest NASCAR Machines.* Berkeley Heights,
    NJ: Enslow Publishers, Inc., 2008.

Web Sites:

NASCAR.COM: Juan Montoya
www.nascar.com/drivers/dps/jmontoya00/cup

NASCAR Sprint Cup: Juan Pablo Montoya
www.racingone.com/driver.aspx?driverid=103&seriesid=1

Glossary

championship: a series of races to decide a winner

contest: an activity to win a prize

helmet: a hard hat that keeps the head safe

Indianapolis 500: a 500-mile (800-km) race held at Indianapolis Speedway

karting: racing in very small cars

Index

CART Championship Series 12, 30
championships 6, 12
children 24, 26
Colombia 4, 24, 30
Daytona Speedway 22
Formula 1 16, 18
formula racing 10, 12, 14, 16, 28
Grand Prix of Monaco 16, 30
helmets 26
Indianapolis 500 14, 30
karting 6
Kart Junior World Championship 8
open-wheel racing 18
open-wheel, single-seat cars 10
Rookie of the Year 20, 30
South America 4, 30
Sprint Cup 20, 30
wife 24, 26